the
man
with
the
gallows
eyes

Poetry for a Poet –
With love X Julia

the man with the gallows eyes

selected poetry
1980 - 2005

billy childish

The Aquarium London

Cover and Woodcuts By Bill Hamper

ISBN 1 871894 87 5

Published by
The Aquarium
Woburn Walk
London
UK

Layout By Darryl Hartley

Printed in Great Britain

Contents

There are those who travel down the broad highways of arrogant ambition; others who make their way by base, servile flattery and fawning; and others employ hypocritical deceit; and there are some who take the way of true religion; but I, drawn by my star, travel down the narrow path of knight errantry, which profession leads me to scorn wealth, but not honour.

Don Quijote
Cervantes

Authores introduction
Successes and distruction

This selection of poetry is taken from 25 years of riting. Looking back my poetry plots a strange course. At 20 I was this bright, damaged kid trying to rite my way out of a concockted hell. I had to deal with my childhood sexual abuse, the mental abuse of my oftern absent, alcohlic father and all the normal crap of no education and no one looking out for me. I was at war with all the hipocrits of art and life, so I was quite out numbered. 1st I had to try to stop hating myself.

Luckerly, I am possessed of an extream sence of humoure that understands that ultimately everything is funny. It is true to say that I considered murder and fantasised about revenge sexual acts but fortunatly didn't indulge in either.

Ive no doubt that listening to myself and painting the way I wanted, riting poetry and playing music, the way I wanted were a balm, all-be-it blud soaked and pusy, and even back then I then felt myself tracked by God.

Making all of my werk on the dole free from the contamination of the art world, littery sects and all the other barstards was slow but the only way for me to feel real. Authentisity, not fashion, has always been my guiding star.

By my late 20's I was planning armed robbery as a means of financing my small press ventures and as a way to publish my novel My Fault. A sawn off shot gun was promised by a fellow riter but never matirealised and I was saved again. I could see a patten forming: I have always been saved from success and destruction; Failer is great indeed and is ultimately the only way to succeed.

At 33, with 3 resentfully consenting girl friends in 3 diffrent locations and a serious drink problem my life and health were starting to disintergrate. It was time to take responsibility and grow myself up or go down for good. I stopped drinking after 15 years of alcohlisim and let 2 of the girl friends go. There followed 7 years of intence psycho therripy, I practiced yoga, read the teachings of Buddha and Christ and went on intensive 10 day budhist retreets.

I now realize that a poets job is to build his myth then destroy it. I often tell people that I am not a painter, I'm not a musician and what sort of an idiot would want to be a poet? I am a father now and reedeamed. I try not to hide, but we all hide. Young riters come to me and show me their wounds and I say - the gutter is a fine place to start from but a shit place to stay - pick up your bed and walk!

red lite road

i seen it in london
kings cross
i seen it in chatham
high street
i seen it in hamburg
3 o'clock in the afternoon

that same orange face
hiden under crusty crud
a girl child
dressed as a big mumma
like giggling geese
in a nicotine rain
their orange compainion curten
hanging lostly with limp love

christ
i feel like some dog
eaten a spoon
maybe i should of talked
a frendly word
it helps any man
(male or female)
just all those faces
on all those streets
looking sick as dogs
prepeared for surgery

**nude encounter
in a dust cart**

soho rendezvous
in a smashed up
police jag
tea creeling round my guts
she offered me
pussy cat tails
that made powdery shadows

a dust cart pulled past
the window shouting –

COME IN AND
DISSCUSS YOUR
SEXUAL PROBLEMS
WITH ONE OF
OUR LOVELY
NUDE MODLES

little monky
make me a pastry man
with currents for eyes
and a little neck tie
little monky
make me a pastry man

a big salami
in the urin trough
bit'n off
she was blind to it
in the end
it tasted so close

the chatham SS

i went to bed with the liveing
dead today
got a bogey on my cheek
stinky socks
shit stains in my pants
n a cheque for fifteen qwid

some of us smiled at a joke
no boidy moved
then one man started screaming
at a black man in the que
'fuck off yu black barstared'
they moved out into the aisle
the silly old git
swinging punchys

people felt sorry for the
black man
but not one of us felt sure
enough to say or do anything
no one felt like they were rite
we were all rong thats why
we were there

id of punched that silly arsed
barstared if my head was any better

when the spunk hits yur in the face

then this bloke says
'yu nans dead' n its the same man
who raped you
then it starts raining
then somebody makes yu nob sore
then all this spunk starts flying atcha

then the bus comes
but it dont go your way
it aint half fare
it just goes up the other side of
the hill n it costs 20p
he says 'its up to you mate'
n i think
i got all the time in the world
spaces to live in big as thirty seconds
as wide as 30 years
no diference all bloody ages
n i say
'ill take it i got to get moveing'

n weer going up and down the hill
n people are haveing babys n dieing
n thats forgeting the fucking n still-
born
n i got off the bus n the rain hit me
hit this page n the wind swept over
my ribs threw my cotten shirt n the
spunk came flying past me some of it
hitting me in the face

fat nature

so whats this nature i heard people
talking about
the children crying about
some sexual nature
some human nature
sqwirrels – murders – perverts nature
a big fat nature for us all

i smoked some naturel cigerets
i drank some naturel wisky
i read some naturel porn

i saw some fucking freek with a beard
n a weetabix jumper waveing a board
above his head
i saw some fucking freek telling the
end of the world

i got into some naturel tv
eat a naturel sossage made from pigs
cock n brains
killed by a naturel man earning his
money
i had a naturel egg layed by a naturel
chicken stuck in a six inch box

n im gonna die naturely
in front of some car
a failed kiddny
brain hemerage
a 60 megaton bomb
every damn bit of it nature

back up the rd

i walked down the road tonite
i saw a mongrel dog
dirty gray n black
he trotted towards me
eyes showing up in the street lite

he was half starved like me
but he was really hungry
we passed each other
i wundered if hed like to take
a kip in my back garden

i went on down the road towards
the phone box

just befor i got there a girl
came out the pub – run up the stone
steps n beat me to it
i lit a cigeret n waighted
she dropped a coin n swore
i heared her say 'i just want the truth'
then she started sobbing
i got embarised n moved off a bit
when she came out she had tears in
her eyes
she smiled at me 'sorry' she said
i thought 'whys she saying sorry to me'
i woundered weather to ask her if she
wanted to come back to my house n sleep
with me
i just said 'thats alrite'
n she went off home – if she had one

i made my call
i diddnt cry
i diddnt want the truth
i wouldnt no it if i saw it
i had another fag n walked back up
the road

when i got no one

when i got no one
i got eyes like screwed up fists
cock cooked in the sun like
a drowned worm
legs like worped wood
head like a block of cheese
hands like wite butterflys
with blue vains
mouth like a laughing pit

when i got no one
i got a girl on my arm
– a bankock whore
i got a message on my bum
– a smart arsed letter
i got holes in my arms
– cigeret holes
n a hang-man above the whore
– a gallows

thats what ive got when
i got no one

dog end of a dog end

i searched round the ash trays
lifted a pice of orange peel
dead matches n ash
i found the but of a but
got some papers
bust the cigs open n rolled the
dry bakie into a snout

bill told me he saw the dog with
three legs moveing up his road
i got a burn on – me – i said -
'ive seen em
wagging their stumps like second
tails
sniffin each other n food bettween
the dustbins
streets with more dogs than people
mad gangs of em atackin children
stealing from the blind
smashing up telephone keosks
drunk on wisky n wine
fuckin our whores and women
the road of meny dogs
dressed in hi heels – face powder
manky fur coats
scampering down the hi street'

i got my fag burning hard
n started on rolling another one
'somethin biting atcha throat
digging up yu garden
crapin on yu boot
look up n theres a three legged
dog wagging his stump atcha'

i bust open what was left of the
but
n added the flakes of dry tobaco
to the new one
i rolled up n sat back puffin
on the dog end of a dog end

letter from a potential psycopath

i stood on the kittens back
and tried to break her back
i held the gold fish in the
palm of my hand till it
wriggled free n fell back
in the bowl
i just couldnt belive it was
alive

i banged my head on the wall
and 4 foot up the bathroom wall
are smashed tiles
but it just kept rattling
round my head
i clubed my hand a 1/2 dozen times
with a 4lb club hamer to get
a week of werk

i made the family dog lick
my cock
i held it in the palm of my
hand then i tossed onto the floor
i strangled the dog till he
stopped breathin
then let him go and he went
and lapped it up with a rasping
noise in his throat

i stood behind my father
clentching an iron poker
grinding my
back teeth

this is normal
i am a healthy 22 year old

will the circle be unbroken

bettween chatham
n waldeslade
we saw – one mongrel -
one dwarf hunchback
2 screaming kids
1 sleeping baby
1 mother – 1 sister in law
n a fuck happy gypo
with a pice of gold
in his ear

im licking the spot
on the edge of my lip
rolling round corners in
a big green buss
we hit a bend
n take a deep hill
down past the hospital
where i was born n
my grandad lies dien

i get off after the hospital
n walk down into luton rd
a couple more big busses
roll past
the heavy sun rolls past
burning down n shooting up
the dirty windows

i smoke a cigeret
test my spot n
hold onto my guts
meanwhile my grandad
lets go of his with a
half empti can of beer
on his bedside cabinet

the can of beer cost
me about 36 $^{1}/_{2}$p

my father aged 5

i ran in there
kicked the door back
n grabbed him
round the throat
i got him over the
sink n then banged
his head aganst the
bottle rack

his face cryed with
no blud in his eyes
or lips
n he was five years
old n 'wouldnt hurt
mummy'

i let him go n then
he was comeing towards
me with his hands
flaping like
dry wite birds
i told him to keep
back n held my fists
up ready

i wasnt going to have
him sneek in there n
knee me in the balls

he walked out

i rang my brother n
told him about it
he seamed to aprove

i diddnt tell him that
he was next

hear i stand

hear i stand
22
one mother – sweet
one father – fucked
one brother – sucsessfull
with an education
as clean and as long
as his arm

hear i stand
22
worts on my cock
'the doctor burned the
ones off my arse'
100 paintings
a couple of hundred
poems
2 dead teeth
gonnarhea n hurpis
i think ive got
excilent qwalifactions

poem

it wasnt a rose
in winter
it was a dirty pice
of tissue cought
in a hawthawn bush
but somehow it was
better than a rose

one of my paintings

one of my paintings
blocks up a hole in
the bathroom
another 3 or 4 make
a barrier to stop the
kittens falling down
stairs

one was once tared
to the roof of a
wearhouse in battersea
to keep the rain out

dont let anyone ever
say that
my art is not usefull

a mad noise like birds

ive got to tell you -
she said -
i diddnt abort that baby
i wouldnt abort that baby
i admit i drank a lot
and wore my belt tight
but i diddnt abort that baby

i lost it 2 days after yu
picked me up by the stomach
and threw me across the floor
im not saying its your fault
i diddnt tell you i was pregnent
becouse i was scared youed
call me irresponsible
but i diddnt abort that baby
- i wouldnt
im not saying its your fault
but i lost it 2 days after
you threw me across the floor
by my stomach

her voise kept going faster
faster and faster
a mad noise like birds

be qwite ... i gasped
be qwite – be qwite

i dont understand how or
what your riteing – she said
- i dont understand why

15 qwid

walking threw lester sq
at 10.35pm
with her hard on
my shoulder

i rip up my last 15 qwid
and sprinkle it over
her head
like
confetti

thats the only type
of weding shes gonna get

the dog

the dog
was
dead
and so was her uncle colin
and
she was
stuck in a lift with her arms
crossed
and
the dog
was licking her all over
and
she was
trying to hit the dog with
her crossed arms

i was standing lookin down
at her and misscheviously
laughin

this was her dream
not mine

my father

my father was absent
my father used to spend 300 qwid
on fucking the fatist uglyist
whores
my father was a drunkerd
my father beat my mother
my father was afraid of his father
my father was a failer
my father was a criminel
my father was unhappy
my father was a mad man

and when i punched him
down stairs
the bruise came up under his
left eye
and crawled down his cheek
like a purple slug

a contented life

maybe if i haddnt
watched my
father drag my drunken
mother upstairs
when i was six

if i haddnt been forced to
sleep those nites with that
46 year old man when i was 9

maybe if i haddnt dressed in
my mothers cloaths and exposed
myself on the street when
i was 10 – then got the family
dog to lick my nob

maybe i could of
spent a
contented life
chipping stone
in the dockyard
or scrapping rottin fruit
from under the convayer belts
in the fruit factory
or
cleaning the shit out of
the bogs
in the mad house

or even become a successful poet
riting on the buti of what?

poem 4 years to late

why dont people
turn screaming mad
why arnt there more
famins and floods
why dont the cars just
drive into each other
and the plains drop
from the sky

the ships should sink
the doors fall off there
hinges
the cups and jugs overturn
the legs fall off chairs
the wings off flys
the legs off dogs

why dont more people
comit murder – rape and
unhappyness
then jump from
burning windows

how can you just
leave me
and outside
the sky wont even rain

the uninvited living

i check the bed and my legs
for fleas
i check my face for pimples
i check my eyes for life
but all i see is dobs of mud
i check the plugs out
i check what ive riten
i check my nob for saws

i check the toiletpaper for shit
i check the shit in the pan
i check my arse for worts
i check my pants and socks
to see if they stink
and they do

i check the doors bolted
i check the pillow for spyders
i check the cups and bath to
i check the tv page in the paper
i check the street for -
young girls – women and madmen
i check the sky for falling plains
i check the nite for -
black dogs – moving blackness
and the uninvited liveing

this madness in my life

poetry and wood

there will be a time when you
are not here to read this
there will be a time when this
earth is blasted back into the
rock from which it was formed

there will be a time -
years and years of countless
seconds -
this world has lived without
us before and it will live
without us again
this is as sure and as
important as the death of a
slug

there will be a time – i no
when there wont be these women
ive acumilated queing to be
fucked
there will be dry years
long dry years and a death
that i can only guess at

there will be a time when im
not driveing threw the nite
on a push bike with no lites
no air in the tiers
drunk on snake bite – guinnes -
wisky and rum with a carrier bag
full of wood blocks depicting a
life

the angel of death

she is 11 and a 1/2
from hull
drinks pepsi cola
likes net ball
her father is a fisherman
was a solder
one set of grandperents
is german
the other swidish
but she speaks
north england
her name is sandra
and her birthday is
september the 10th
when she is 12
her father will take her
on a fishing boat
for a 2 week trip

i talk to her at
the bar
me – double gin
her – pepsi cola

and her mother looks on
like the angel of death

no reason

'there must be a reason'
she said
'theres no damn reason'
i said
'but i-want-to-be-loved'
she sobbed
'go suck a pigs teet'
i said
'2 years'
she said
'2½
i said
'ooooooh'
she said
'hell'
i said
'but i want sex and i
only want it with you'
she said
'big deal'
i said
'ive unloaded my missery
onto you
and youve unloaded your
missery onto me
and now theres nothing left
but missery – its finished'
i said

p.s. i was rong
there is allways more missery

rochester castle

it is half 2
in a saterday
morning in mid-
november

i have drunk
enough for 2
and fallen off
my push bike
twise

there is a
heavy frost
and i am lien on
my back in the
hard grass

i can see orion
and the dog star
and a shooting star
scratches across
the nite sky

blacker than
the nite
the shadows of
the castle
towering upwards

empty and dead
a monument
to our youth
our past

it saw siege
bludy war
laughing victory
and grining
defeat

and beneath
the foundations
are the graves
of earlyer
fortifications

forgotten peoples
there pashions
and battles
buried
buried well

1000 years and
beyond
now redused
to a mear
tourist atraction

it would seam better
if this castle too
could no the
decency of a
quiet grave

i once worked at
the top of those
towers
clinging to the
scafold
reworking the
damp stones

now i am a drunk
counting the
stars

rochester bridge (evening)

the stench of the river down here
and the stillness of the ebb-tide
the gulls scream and the traffic
rolls past over the heavy shouldered
bridge
comeing from somwhere and going
somewhere
and the sun a pale disc echoed in
water

the evening mist makes this scene
somehow primevil
i can imagin this river without man
old and resilient
the esplanade laid waste to the
flood-plain
the hillside wiped clean of human
development
the little boy houses washed clean
away

but the little boats rest at anchor
and the london traffic buzzes over
the distent stain of the M2 bridge
the gulls
the water
the oil scum
an alcoholic waves to me
i recognise him
wave back

the nobel beast

i no that riting this down
dosent mean anything
or change anything
poetry is riten by fools
for fools
at best it is lame and half-
witted
and at worst a self-important
word game
but also
spooning half a bag of suger
into a cup of hot watery milk
and coffee and eating a pile of
re-heated chips with a half-
bottle of ketchup dose little
for the soul
nor does
mowing lawns or worrying about
the rong people smokeing the
rong cigerets in the rong places
or the stock-markets up
or the stock-markets down
or the stock-markets gone fucked
its self
or buying the weeks shopping
or new cars
or washing machines
or those invisable stains
or kicking a biro into a 63 year
old mans left ear
or selling real estate
or hifis

or cageing animals or humans
or emptying other peoples rubbish
or certifying them insain
and filling there arms with detergent
or selling virginal deoderent
or tooth picks
or carwash
or catching dogs
or gassing dogs

no man can convince me
that any of theses things are
exactly loaded with some great
nobility or dignity

we are these people

like an herominus bosh
prophecy
the orange puke of
the street lites lite up
the sky over these towns

staining the clouds with
the fake scum of dawn
and beyond the city limits
other towns echo
that same dream

but no fish-headed
monsters here -
only humens in massed
populations
ugly unthinking indervidueIs
moveing in there sick
social orders

vidios pop music and
telivision are the opiates
theres no religion here
but
we do pray
we pray for more
and if we believe
we believe
like monks without god

i am a despret man

i am a despret man
with despret hands
lack of education
and bad teeth

watching cars move by
people putting food into
their mouths
and waking up in a
hamburg bed with a
woman whos name i
have forgotten
thinking of a hot sun
yellow fields
some crows
a man drinking terpentine
and a single gunshot

treading ice water
mid-atlantic
the feeling almost gone
and some bobbing dead
who knows that poetry
is a small wite room
with small wite death

bunching an empti dress
in my hands holding
it to my face
and laughing

early spring

a glass of good cheap wine
an early spring
sitting carving wood in my
back yard 1/2 6 in
the evening

the radio plays classical
the news talks of people
as if they were gods
or dreams
personalities
politicians
those who think
they know how others
should lead their
lives
i take a swig of wine
on my government course for
the long term
unemployed
gold teeth grinning
sitting
on old newspapers
sending the glittering woodchips
spraying out over the butifully
embroidered concrete

father

i wrestled him down
on to the setee and
explained to him
that people could never
understand that although
we fight we still love
each other

then i got him under
the desk and dug his
eyes out of his head
with a screw-driver

his head is a sheet
of metal and his 6 eyes
are brass tacks

zoo

on a sunny autumn afternoon
we traveled to london
and paid our money
we saw the chimpansees
their women were on heat
the arses pink
and extended
like blocks of meat
the old chimp sniffed at them
and showed them his stiffy
and the schoolgirls giggled

we moved on to the
orang-utang enclosure
theyve got these hands
big sad hands
great hands
and skirts of orange/brown hair
the male checked the womans
cunt under her tresses
he parted the folds and sniffed
then he looked out at us
primevil
human
yes!
undoubtedly human
and
his woman did the same
and
i felt foolish being there
staring dumbly with the crowds
sucking on our ice-creams

gentle men of
gentle books
know this:

forgive me my dear
if my smile is cracked
ive been at war
these 30 years past

forgive me
if i
demand
atack!
demand
atack!

but when you take
up
the axe
it grows hard
to let it
down and
in the end
it cums easyer
to make war
than peace

forgive me that i
find it
hard to give
easy to take
war not love
formed me

ive been at war
these 30 years past

fighting my family
my lovers
the fools
the heros
the teachers
the bosses
and
the unemployed

rank upon rank
of the barstards
eyes grinning
but
never falling
all
those
who know better
how others should
live their lifes

forgive me my dear
that im not a
gentle man
of gentle books

like children drunk

the pub is not good
but
at least it isnt
the house

and
the return
stairing into
shavin mirrors
over
the scum of the
sink
and
recognising nothing

our mugs empty
and
like 14 year old
kids
we
kiss the cold mirrors
mouth
dreaming of feeling

that strange bravery

the painting

thats what its
all about
doing that
god-thing
on
the canvas

trying to glue
the world
together
with
septic egos
and
grand vanitys

to believe
totally
in
the importance
of your work
but
no
that alls
to he rubbed
out
in 2 life times
or less

thats the
balancing act
shouldering self
importance
with the humbling
ferocity
of the stars

there lies that
strange
bravery

and the thing
the kid
wasnt
even
sobbing in
life

she told me she was
pregnant
10 weeks
shit!

i looked to her
pleading eyes
and already i was
riting the poem

how id visit after
the abortion
taking flowers
not for the dead but
for the living

i held her near
placing my palm to
her poor belly
feeling for the thing
inside
the egg that was never
to taste
bitter love
sea-salt tears
nor know
the glorious sun-rayed
flowers
and the blazing faces
of the living

to taste nothing
but the mothers blud
then back to
the sod
to roar back to
the ashes
to the dust of all
beginnings
and all
ends

like a fool

puffing on poison
and
downing gut-rot

like a fool
judging fools

my last tenner
on a
bottle of jamaica
rum

craving
unashamedly for
people to like
me
to be seduced
by my crummy
lines

but most of all
the women
to suckle the
breast
and
lose myself
whence i came

i remember
being 5 or 6
years of age

and
3 elder girls
10 or 11
leading me by
my hand
across the
mudflats of
this damned estuary
me with
butterfly net
in hand
seeking to catch
the red-backed
crabs
which made
the girls run
screaming
and
gigling
but always returning
to hold
my little hand

admiring
of my youth
of
my purity

and
like a damned
fool
i want them
to lead me
again
forever

pure as spring water

we were lyin in bed
the sheets hot and wet with
our bodys
the sunlte coming in
some birds singing

- i am as pure as the
purist spring water

and as i speak i can feel
its true
my mind a fine edge
undirtyed as a childs

- you aint pure your full
of diseases

and she goes to hit me
i hold her arms back and
roll my waight onto her
she struggles and i laugh
in her face
she spits at me

- you make me sick
i told you i diddnt want
you to bring me anything
back from germany
but you brought me
girlfriends and gonnarea

i look down into her twisted
mouth but nothing can spoil
my mood
i carnt feel angry i can
only laugh pure peals of
laughter
pure as the purist spring
water

woodblocks and this poem

outside my window is the poor
frozen city
cars wont start – chaos!
water pipes burst – catastrophy!
the poor humans are in turmoil

i piss in the frozen toilet downstairs
then leave my home
i walk away from my work
(woodblocks and this poem)

i spend 3 days or more away
i get drunk on my social security
check
after the wisky maybe ile walk
myself back here in the dead of
nite without my knowing

next morning hungover
and the
toilet downstairs still held
in its block of ice
but the werk is done
something is fixed in words or
wood

this is my method
im not talking about jigsaw
puzzels or lituary traditions
im talking about sneeking up on
your own soul

being 10 years old

n shouting as hard
as you can
hopeing to lose
your voise
wanting to be a
tranosorous-rex
or a squirrel
n 2 weeks holidays
at seasalter
n allways hanging
round the pub doorway
till gone 11
n the grown-ups feeding
us on pop n crisps
n odd coppers for
the one-armed bandits
n allways being shoved
by that barstard brother
of mine
till it was chuckin-out
time
n wed all head back
to the shack
n us kids with so much
brass in our pockets
we could hardly hold
our shorts up

n in the carpark nearly
losing my thumb in the
slam of uncle normens
car door
n him pattin my arse
n grining down at me thru
his evil little specks
n me allready shitting
meself
knowing that when we
got back
id have to wank his
cock

like a god i love all things

her name was toshie
- and what dose toshie
mean?

i asked her
- given quickly and
sensitivly
she tells me

and i laughed and over
the year we became lovers
(only i am no lover)

her 25 years old and never
given to another man
- but how do you feel?
she asks me

- you never tell me how
you feel... do you love
me?

and just that word love
makes sadness step from
my mouth and i think

of course i love you
like a god i love all
things

fire
fire
fire

allways thinking of fire
n stinking of bonfires
n burnt fingers
n singed eye-lashes
n smoking dry hollow weeds
n spitting out earwigs
or 10 cadets
or 10 woodys
or 5 park drive
or just an old dog-end
and
allways having at least
3 matches n a bit o strike
in yu pocket

n setting bush-fires
burning out whole corn fields
of jap snipers
and
burning kevin hardin at the
stake
only cutting the roap
as the flames licked up past
his laces

and
the cans of liter fuel
n setting lite to yu own hand
seeing how long yu can stand it
till you have to shake out the
blue flames

n drippin wax on yu hands
3 candels-worth making a wax
glove

n then guy fawlks
n chuckin lited bangers in
the water barrel
n letting bangers off in yu
hand
n bustin em open n making
genies
n making our own gun powder
n weed killer bombs
n just burning anything that
would fuckin well burn

banging the clay from my knees

my girlfriend
was eating codine
and i was in
the park fuckin
this big-titted
18 year old whore

i got her to sqwat
over me sos i could
lick her arshole
then her lien on
her back
and
these tits just
hanging down
either side
of her arm-pits
resting on the
ground
i had to scoop
them up and hold
them between my
thighs and wank
myself into her
mouth

n she gets up
walks to the bushes
and spits it out
me stood there
wiping myself
n banging the clay
from my knees

-i havent washed
for 2 weeks
she says
i hear the venom in
her voise

-good
i say
-good

the little brave ant

a little black ant
has joined me
at table
sucking from tiny
pools of spilt
beer

somhow i feel for
this little
brave one
me wielding pen
and
puffing brimstone

the house is dark
and empity now
just the two of us
joined for this
moment
comrades in drink

your golden hair

that hot still summers
day
when we swam out
till a half mile off shore
then let the slowly
incoming tide carry us
back shoreward

and
we noticed hundreds of
tiny spyders
thousands of them
walking the sufis
tension
only being capsised
by the ripples we made
whilest treading water

it dosnt seam much now
but back then it did
it seemed like a
miricle

and
the 20 or so i saved
lifted by my wet fingers
to your golden hair
that way

the moth

a stark buti will provail when this earth
is scorched clean of the two-legged ones
a stark buti little moth
a stark buti with no fool of a poet to utter it

and meanwhile i hear dark mutterings
voices of insects
and
the fucking of butterflys

the hoverfiy is not a wasp
and you beetle
like a black thumbnail
go back to the woods and rest your
overstuffed head

here let bitterness evaporate (amsterdam 92)

here
where i drink beer and discover
a hole in the soul of my left boot
and later the delicate imprint of a kings crown
and the date 1942 stamped on each ankle

here
by the canal where the water runs foul
the jokes are obvious and the laughter hollow

here
with a waterside beer my loved one by my side
and a sun that scorches holes in impossible
shields

here
where we are free to buy luxsorys
and dream freedom

here
where the unexpected glimps of tasseled
hair licking at the barmaids dampend armpit
makes the lips test salt

here
where the women use their bodies like knifes
and the men turn their lust inwards
and swallow gutloads of bile

here
where children play
bottles clink
and young men are made ready for war

here
where if love would but come to the
loveless and peace to the whores
then so too would lite to the marbled
eyes of the blind
and gentleness come bubbling like a
clear undeniable spring

of violence and solitude

it is time to reclaim
the mechanism of life
to de-feather and finger the guts
of small animals
and
wonder at the ticking lives
of insects
to grow wretched and to understand

to caress the emptiness
to dip my snow-like hands in
the lifes flower of anothers blud
to caress the loaded gun
and anoint the good arrow

i require the action and the
purpose to punch
to bludy friends noses
and to understand the glory
of violence
to find that man part of me
which desires to taste blud and
know the kill
a baptism of gore to balance
this hot head and timidity of fist

i will go rest my troubled brow
on the bows of ancient oaks
sap strength undiluted from
lifes source
and
pray to the ghost of that
magical blackbird i gunned down
aged 12 years old
pausing to put another pellet in
its feared eye
that black deed which compounded
a childhood of bad luck

remember the forgotten

10 pink toes
10 pink little toes
and one crushed and all askew

where be her hands now
where her hart and hair
the braided and the combed
where be her teeth and tongue
speaking with others now
uttering foreign names

and on the mantle piece
2 hair bands lay discarded just as
she left them
2 golden hallowed child-like things
a hair still twisted remembering the yellow
shock of her head

remember the forgotten sorrowed man
hold trinkets in your palm
pick thru these desperate remains
bow your head and kiss the wounds

kiss the damp hairs
kiss her thighs
kiss her feet
10 pink toes
10 pink little toes
and one crushed and all askew

the bitter cup (song)

and i remember the breath of my father
his kisses were bearded and damp
the romance of the bottle dragging him down
to awaken disheveled in the tank

and theres no sea deeper than the piss of the bottle
and none speaks the truth like the drunk
wisky runs thru me like a sorrowful river
im down on my knees and im sunk

and i remember my mother hitting the gin
she fell and we thought she was dead
naked and doll-like
his skull face was shouting
we ran to our room painted red

hot for women we curse and abuse them
they say we aint got no respect
full of bravado godless and fearfull
we pray no one will detect

and theres no taste sweeter than the rush of hot vomit
seived thru decaying back teeth
id wisper i love you
and quit all his hating
but in truth i aint got the belief

smashed and disheveled
of course they did wreck us
poisoned by our own bitter cup
stumbling and hoping inside i was lonely
im sick and im down and
im drunk

donkey

and i remember there was always
a field with a sunny corner
and a donkey who would lift his
sorrowful head and walk painfully
over to us
to be patted and fed grass thru
the wire
big velvet ears twitching and a coat
like an old worn carpet
and there was a sky big and blue
and my father saying it was time
to go

and there was a pig-sty on a hill
in a gale
and three piglets escaped under
the wire
and us kids wearing shorts and scraped
knees chasing them in circles thru
bushes and up and down ancient
wooden steps

and there was always a secret camp
over the back and a fire with
field mushrooms a tin of beans
and baked apples
and there was rain and mud
and wet grass
jumpers smelling of woodsmoke
and believing in the wilderness beyond
we were as feared of the fox
as the wolf
and i stroked the donkey

and also i have felt god

because i have stared down
the infinity of the wisky bottle
and seen children hands waving
and heard the empty voices
of the lost

because i have named lovers
on both fists and kissed with
my tongue the arses of girls like
the stars of god
because i have hated myself more
than is decent for any man to hate
and still i bite down

because i still feel for my fathers
hand gone these 27 years past
and the trees fall like hartbeats
in the nite

because missery drips like clocks
and the sun shines with yellow fingers
and my hart bursts still with unknown
fires

because i have stared down these
bleak moments
i write this

in the palm of my youthfull hand

i have a photograph of us standing
together
she is laughing with her front teeth
blacked in
only there not blacked in theyre in
my pocket
and im grining dragging on a cigeret

brave boy
you have her plate in the palm of your
youthfull hand
and shes standing there teetering on her
5 inch steletos
waving her arms about like some sad
fucking whore
and your grining with bravado
a brave boy who considered both rape
and murder as reasonable options

a brave boy struggling for manhood
feared of women and resentfull of their
power over you
a brave boy scared to step
cowed in the shadow of small stark
violence

and of course you were found wanting
and
you grin and blow smoke in the face
of the winners

and the joke is
is that all along youve got her crooked
smiling teeth in your pocket
and your both grining in this sad funny
photograph

summer slugs

each morning i rise
rake out the grate
kindle a fire
and make porridge

and here by my foot
lies a slug
trodden in the nite
his guts spilt

such a low belly
and no modisty

- where is your shell
dumb slug?
you have left
your
hat at home

and opening a fresh
packet of salt
i pour a barrier round
the busted skirting board
and across the doorstep
to the back yard

i am telling them
- beware!
keep out!
go forage in the lush
un-mown lawn
in the hedgerow i leave
un-cut for you
in the cats piss and dog rose
dont tread your nite trails
dumb slug
for here be giants

primary school tough

there was frost on the tarmac
that december morning
and my cap was pillarbox red
badged with acorns and sat
upon my blond head
and
i walk in long grey socks
and hand-me-down shorts
of my brother
my fathers tie knotted at
my throat

it was decembeer the first 1964
and little andrew walked proudly
by my side
and to every passing person
would announce
- this is my friend steven
he is five years old
today

thumb print

i wore an american sailors cap
and cupped my hands to my
snaggled teeth as i grinned in
this photo he clicked

a 9 year old kid handled
by this 40 year old man
his unkind grasp
and fake friendliness still
walk in my sleep
his thumbprint indellible
upon my childs spine

and i would like to ask
but one question of you father
of you mother

- where were you my brave
protectors?

and i see you kissing in other
peoples arms
in cheap bars
oblivious
loving only your own pain

soho 1972

i walked with
a childs face
with blond yellow hair
teeth fucked
and chest buckled
with fear

and a businessman
with briefcase and glasses
crosses the road in front of me
turns his mangled face and says
- this is a sexy place
isnt it?

the names of those ive wished dead

today is the day
to tell of my undisclosed
desire for power
to mention that i have
had sex with a dog
and to utter the names
of those ive wished dead

today is the day
of all the insects
ive tortured
to open my cupped hands
and let go the ants
the wasps and the flies

today is the day
of all the women ive loved badly
to open my delicate heart
and speak of this fear
of women
of spyders
and the night

today is the day
i breathe of my sorrow
hold myself in my arms
with pitty
and admit that others live
that they too must be free
to set their own paths
thru hell

the silent knowledge of ants

there are mice on the streets
mice in the gardens
and mice in the kitchen
weve heard their scratching
and seen their little black shits

they wring their pink hands
and with quick eyes
watch us from beneath
the busted cooker

they have attached themselves
to our minds and our habits
and the slugs come too
with the silent knowledge of ants

they step night trails
and with invisible eyes
watch us from beneath
the busted cooker

and so we all remain
and so we all make bed
with peabugs and spyders
and the silent knowledge of ants

dead funny

i am a thorn in the side
of the establishment

my success annoys everyone
to the extent that even i pretend
not to be successful

my adolescent concerns
are the bore of the town
my friends hiss at me
and ex-lovers wish me dead

honestly even my own mother
cant bear to read my texts

it seems ive painted a lot of shit
so much so that i meet complete strangers
who presume that i swim in it with glee

and with every poem i rite
my fame grows
another nail in my coffin
people feel embarrassed for me
everything i utter becomes a cliche

when oh when the people ask
will billy shut up

waterloo station

ive been ill
i was ill all last year
i split up with chris
i had an abortion
it was twins and
they cut them up inside
of me
and two days later
a little arm came out
whilst i was sitting
in the taxi
but i wont tell you
about it cos youll
only go and blab about it
in one of your stupid poems

she glared at me
hungry and broke
and i understood
that what i loved about
this woman
was the depth of her spite
and anger
she hated the world
she hated men
and she hated me

i handed her a twenty
and watched her stupid
face light up

shell remember all of my
indiscreditions
but never the gift
of this poem

the billy childish

i am billy childish
ex drunk
and compulsive masturbator
late nite vomiter of good liquor
kisser of purple lipped women
riter of poems celebrating the
emptiness of my love
poems hungering for the moment
of my passion
wishing it could always be so
to never let my cock fall

i am billy childish
ex strongman
and 2-bit lover
late nite namer of names
corrupter of the literate
riter of poems that dare
to dream to pass down
the centurys
and touch the harts of the
the yet-to-be-born
wishing to hold them
to my arms
and kiss them all

i am billy childish
ex-poet
and failed suiside
late nite vomiter of truth and lies
kisser of the arses of girls
like the stars of god
riter of poems to lick
the thighs of the dead
for ex- lovers to denounce
and teachers to hate
wishing to paint my life
and to never let my
voice quieten

the 5 pound note tree and the tyranical dandy

this poetrys grave stuff
no kidding
i read my old poems
and nearly die of shame

what a poor little bleeder!
as if i was never 17
and diddnt swing like a monky
between the lamposts of chatham town

my father
(who incidently
had all of his suits hand taylored
by mister driver of newcombs
shirt makers to the king)
was a tyranical dandy
and unmittigatted shit
of quite devistating preportions
allways dressed to the nines
a crease rite up his arse!
theres style for you
style of yesteryear

- presentation is what counts!
that was his maxim
that and
-money dosnt grow on trees!

as if it could
a 5 pound note tree in full bloom
amongst the ornimental cherrys
on new road rochester
its buitifull blue blossoms
dripping onto the blond heads
of laughing children

a sad donky
and a fat man smiling

speaking as a man who doesnt eat cheese
and who paddled into 2nd place in the
kent schools under-18s slalom 1975
(three entrants only)

speaking as a man who doesnt own a television set
doesnt read daily papers
and the radio remains clicked to off

speaking as a man with twelve fillings
four verucas
and one o'level (art grade A) walderslade secondry
school for boys 1976

speaking as an artist of dubious merit
and the writer of lewd verses

speaking as a man who caught paul wellers plectrum
thrown into the audience at battersea town hall
jubilee week 1977 (support group the boys)

speaking as a man who carved the reclining admiral
and van gogh without a moustache
apprentice stone mason
her majestys dockyard chatham 1976

speaking as a man who wore second hand shoes
up untill he was 33

speaking as a man who tried to run down johnny rotten
on the pavement outside the roebuck public house kings
rd
london 1978 (drunk in charge of a push bike)

speaking as a man with eyes the shape of little fishies
the hands of my father and somebody elses legs
i see that truth only comes staggering up the mountain
side
like a sad donky teetering under the weight of a fat man
smiling

failer

my father has been praticing his suisides again
and failing missrably
his wife calls me
he has taken two overdoses in the last two days
and crys that he wants to die
apparently he stole her car and went on a drunken
death ride
with my six year old brother

it was exactly the same story when i was a kid
me sat trapped in the front seat of his car
and his white hands flailing drunkenly with the wheel
i staired at him sideways
his drooling lips and his beared damp with whisky

we overtook a truck on the brow of waterworks hill at
120 mph
- can we go slower please dad
- you are a child steven and you know nothing!
i was changing your bludy nappys and
my god the stink! and you
wouldnt shut up bludy crying then!

he wrote off three cars in three seperate crashes
and emerged with nothing but a pair of bruised knees
whole sections of motorway crash-barrier were ripped
up
everytime the doctors checked him over and
shook there heads with disbelith
they couldnt belive his luck- not a scratch on him
and then he took an overdose in sight of nurcy and they
took him out to have his stomach pumped

always he has fluffed every golden oppotunity

31st august 1997

why must children go to school?
why must they learn to read and rite?
what is the correct way of roasting a goose?

is meditation benificial?
what exactly is fear?
is it like sex?
is it really so very wrong to drink battery acid?
why shouldn't you clean out childrens ears with a
bent nail?
is murder a tottal aboration?
and if so should people be exicuted for it?
what is it like to be a spyder?
and do they really see out of all eight eyes at once?
whats it like to run about like a wood louse?
is it good for you?
or is it better to jump up and down like a flea?

what use is sience to us if it cant ansewer
these simple but pertinent qustions?
it seams that everybody talks about death
but nobody understands what being dead really means

every grain of rice

what if every body
started riting poetry?
thered be no bludy idiot
left to listen

if every barstard
was bissy painting pictures
thered be no fucker
in the art gallarys
the museums
would grind to a halt
and
thered be no bastard
left to wander around
gauping at it all

if everybody
enjoyed a good heathy sex life
the pornography industry
would collapse over nite
millions would be made redundent
and
the streets be swarming
with the homeless
and
dis-possesed

if only people would
stop to think befor
undertaking
such rash
and
irrasponsibe actions

remember
each and every grain of rice
has its own soul
and
a destiny

a personal history

i hunt death
like a black spyder
like it is a black spyder i mean
a black spyder that i hope
and pray i will not find

what im trying to say is
that i hunt truth
like it is a black spyder
seen
scurrying between a stack
of old bricks
in my fathers back yard

chatham town welcomes desperate men

welcome the nite whatchman
the floor polisher
the dole-que boy
and
the policeman in the rain

welcome the salesman who never sells
the dentist who hates teeth
the docker with out a dock
and
the robber of car hub-caps

welcome lovers who can not love
lickers of bright green ice lollies
motherless children
and
the smashers of car wing mirrors

welcome achne
toothache
kabab shop owners
used-car salesmen
and
the buyers of second hand fridges

welcome the salor from a far away land
and try not to punch him on the nose
welcome pimps prostitutes
and
a smiling dose of the clap

welcome lager drinkers
with tattoed fists
and the bare nuckle fighters of
kent
irland
romany
and
beyond

welcome the uneducated and the lost
welcome teachers to sceared to teach
welcome office werkers
wild 3 legged dogs
and
the smiling of hell

welcome cigaret smokers
hash smokers
pen pushers
stollen car drivers
garage attendents
shelf stackers
shelf haters
heroin users
and
girls in white calf length boots

welcome the men of middle managment
their bored housewifes
and
alcoholic children in private schools

welcome till girls with love-bites

welcome gray skys and icy winds
welcome magpies and crows
welcome con-men and the conned
and
children with flick-knives

welcome men in envy
town planners
councilers of little faith
and
old ladies in faded blue coats

welcome estate agents bearing
false gifts
and dressed in fake pin-stripe suits

welcome the owners of lawns
car show rooms
impossable morgages
and
bank managers who can no longer manage

welcome the indebted and the owners of naught

welcome one eyed cats
and panthers in the nite
welcome circus tricksters
casueal laboures
and crawling curb crawlers

welcome liers
cheats
and
fornicators
welcome poets smiling thru their teeth
welcome dead novelists and
sunken battle-ships
welcome men in blazzers from napal

from the tax office of limehouse reach
to the dole que of the brook
chatham town welcomes desperate men
it loves you all
and
honeres you all

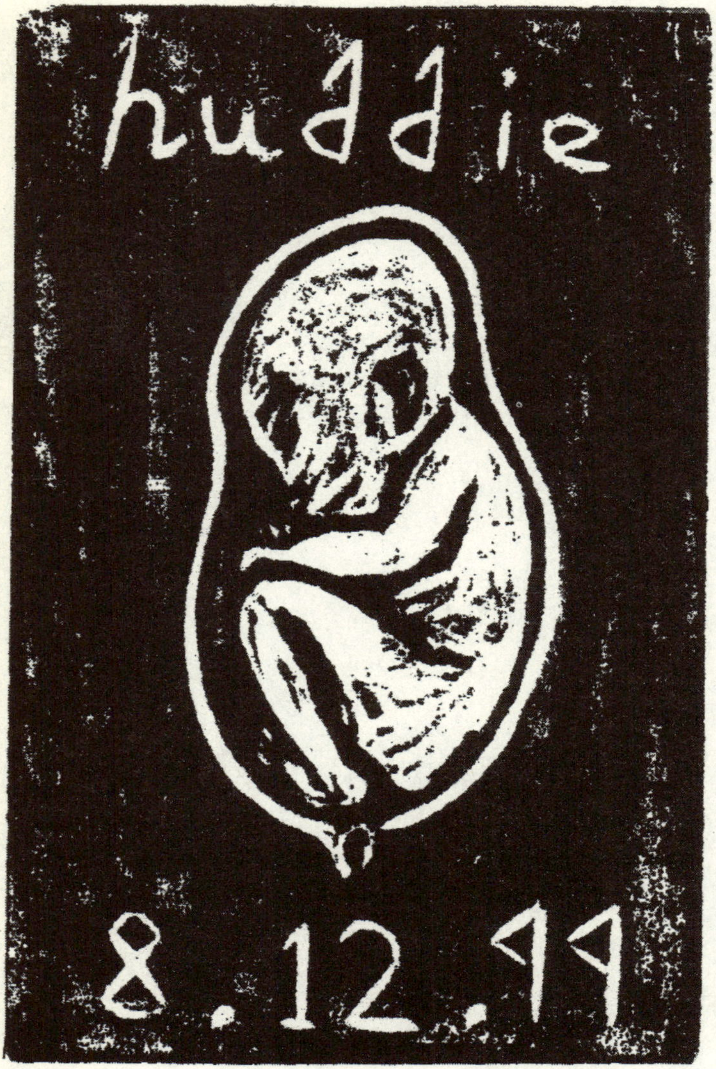
huddie
8.12.99

huddie
8.12. 99

huddie
i may be the strangest father
but i welcome you
your grandmothers welcome you
your grandfathers welcome you
your brothers
and your sisters welcome you
we all welcome you
you belong here

huddie
after 14 years me and keerah decided to part
the last nite we slept togther
was the nite you were conceved
we diddnt chose you
you chose us
and we rejoiced

but for 4 months
we didnt even know you were in there
when keerah finnaly found out
she was pregnent
i got down on my knees
and kissed her belly
- hello i said
- i know a lot of strange
things have been going on out here
but theyer nothing to do with you
you are still wanted
you are welcome

and
5 months later
on a cold morning in december
i arrived at the hospital
wearing my hat and clutching carrier bags
and
a flask of hot tea
i entered the room
keerah was sat astride a chair in labour
i put down my bags
kissed her
then walked to the window
4 stories up
i looked out over this bleak river
a rain-swept veiw from rochester to hoo
and
below us tucked under the hillside
my ugly home town

i suddenly recognise why i have remained
stuck in this landscape when the rest of my family
have long since qwit it
my brother has qwit it
my father has qwit it
and my mother to
im the only one to remain
cept my grandperents
who lay buirid in these chalk hills

for how many thousands of years
have i looked out over this muddy estery?
since befor the romans came?
- certanly
i see myself as a worrior chieften
born here again and again
deposed by romans
deposed by my own clan
fighting to keep my footing
aganist slimy betrails
so i am caught by this land
by the siloet of these familiar hills
my family may run
but im the one who has been left here to desolve the past
and put these ancient ghosts to rest
and you
sweet huddie
who have been my son many times before
are ment to be here with me

me and keerah diddnt bring you into being
you willed yourself into being
this warrior chief has just been waighting for your return

your mother is a brave woman
huddie
she made a butiful plan for you to be born at home
in the most simple way
to incence burning
and
holy music playing

but instead you came into this world arse first
and the doctors wanted to drug her and cut you from
her belly
but your keerah insisted on giving birth and letting you
decide when your entrance should be
she refused all drugs
wishing to keep your blud pure

as her time drew near
i helped her up onto the table
the doctor came and shone a lite
which i fancied was to bright
then i saw your bum sat
deep in keerahs virgina
5 little wite toes

shortly
2 surgons came to view
this strange flemish woman who refussed
all pain releaf
and lieing there on her back
she lifted her head
and
ordered them to leave the room
then suddenly a whole foot appeared
and
the doctor grasped your legs
and
pulled till i thought he would snap you
in two
quickly your back showed purple
it seamed you were already born
but then your head stuck fast

i mopped keerahs brow
and
the doctor gave her a nasty snip
took up his forceps
and pulled you out like a skinned rabbit
he
plopped you
there on to keerahs wite belly

- i have a baby gasped keerah
and
i staired at you in wounder

is it really possable that we all come into this world
in this same way?
murderers
bus conductors
tax collectors
and
saints?
how can one being be alive in another?

- my baby!
i have a baby! keerah sobbed again
and we loved you huddie
with such intencity
the same as we loved you when we first learned
that you were hiding
in keerahs womb

i held you in my arms
as they stiched keerah painfully together again
and spoke with you
letting you know that everything was alright
telling you all those things
that i had once longed to here

you are so butiful huddie
you came into this world
to teach me love
and
i welcome you

you will not be abused
as i was abused
i will not allow it
you will not be told you are ugly
as i was told i was ugly
or that you are backwards or stupid
if you are slow to riting or mathmatics
then damn riting and mathmatics
you will not be told you cryed too much
or that you were too clingy or needy
as i was told i cryed too much
and was too clingy and needy
love cannot spoil a child
if you wish to sing then you shall sing
if you wish to dance then you shall dance
and you will not be told you have a god-awful voice
or that you are tone deaf
or that you have 2 left feet
your desire to be will be your reason to be

yes huddie
you are honered and adored as a child born
i may be the strangest father
but i welcome you
your grandmothers welcome you
your grandfathers welcome you
your sisters welcome you
and your brothers welcome you
you belong here
and
i will allways be here for you

only poets piss in sinks

it is a cold seattle nite
- i cant be bothered to get out of bed
and go all the way to the toilet
i tell her

- its only out thru the kitchen
she tells me

- if im at home i just open the window
and piss into the back yard
she lifts her head from the pillow
and holds me with her dark eyes

- really? she says
my ex-boyfriend would never
do a thing like that

- no? i ask
- no he was very fastidious
and would never piss out of a window
- i dont allways piss out of windows
i correct her
- sometimes i piss in the sink instead

she looks at me
- well he certanly wouldnt do that either
she says
- why not?
i ask
- he just wasnt raised that way
she says levelly
- well nor was i
- then why do you do it?
i think for a second
- becouse im a poet!
i ansewer
then laugh into the pillow

i am the strange hero of hunger

my girlfreind lives
on the other side of the world
and
has
started
reading
crime and punishment
by fydor dostoyevski

- do you recognise the main charicter?
i ask her excitedly
- dosnt he remind you of me?

- ive only just begun
she ansewers
whats his name?

- rodya
but all the charicters
have about 3 diffrent names
i always get confussed
and
cant tell who is who
becouse im dislexic and dont make sounds for the names
but rodya is for short
and
his sister is called dunya
isnt dunya a butiful name?
if little huddie had been born a girl
we would of named her
dunya

when i talk of the buti
of girls names
or the strange bravery
of artists
or see
the lite change
over sea
and sky
every second impossable showers of
gold
turning to terrible hues of purple
and
black
and
my
hart rate quickens
becouse
i am amongst
my
own
people

i am
the hero of all my favorite novels
i live in them
and they
live in me
i am arturo bandini
on angels flight
swearing at a butiful dark haired girl
in tattered shoes

i am rodya
guilty of a terrible and senceless murder
on the streets of st petersburg
i am the strange hero of hunger
starving to spite myself in chrisitiana
i am johan nagel
tormentor of the midget
and suiside
i am ishmail
knocker off of tall hats

i am every novelist
and
every charicter ever dreamed
i am everyone of my favorite artists
and
i feel myself not one jot less
but equell to all of them
turner
munch
holbine
and
hokusi

naturally i have no heros
i am my heros
i am my brothers
and sisters
i feel myself joined by the soul
with all buti
my hart sings with every brave endevor
with the strange wings of impossable butterflys
with every rock that breaths life into this world

i stand shoulder to shoulder with
all denoucers of meaness
i honour spirit and faith
and i uphold the glorious amiture
i am in love with desperate men
with desperate hands
walking in 2nd hand shoes
serching for god
and
hearing god
and hating god
i am a desperate man buckled with fear
i am a desperate man who demands to be
listend to
who demands to connect
i am a desperate man who denouces
the dullness of money
and status
i am a desperate man who will not bow down to
acolayed or success

i am a desperate man who loves the simplisity of
painting
and hates gallarys and white walls
and the dealers in art
who loves unreasonableness
and hot headedness
who loves contradiction
hates publishing houses
and
also i am vincent van gough
hiroshige
and every living breathing artist
who dares to draw god
on this planet

huddie poem
(about lien in the blud soaked towles
cradling you in my arms)

straight after you were born
huddie
they stiched keerah back up
and took her to be cleaned up

i just went for a quick piss
and was coming back down
the corridoor
when they weeled her
passed me
- huddies in the little crib
she called to me as they pushed her
through the swing doors
- his all on his own!

i entered the theatre
(which was now in darkness)
blud heavy towls lay on the derlivery table
and all the machines were switched off
you were curled silently in the plastic crib

i went over and lifted you into my arms
and kissed you my darling huddie
then carried you carefully to the table
were i climbed up
and slept with you to my breast

i no longer love poisonus women huddie
i seek gentleness not pain
i no longer drink from the wisky bottle
like its a gushing tit
i no longer hate my father
or my brother
or my family
no huddie
i am infused with love
infused with life and you
and thats where they found us
asleep amongst the blud and juce of your birth

evidence against myself

envious of everybody
i give unessassary information
that incriminates myself
if i find a speck of dirt in my hart
i hold it up for all the world to see
this does nothin
but damage my own cause
i am a criminal
i am greedy
and hide everything

i am vengful and jelliose
and

watching people win
sets my teeth on edge
i push too the front
and allways
have to have more than
the man stood next to me

my mother says
that i
am marching in my fathers footsteps

she also points out
that
i am contancurus and argumentative
by nature
will not listen to reason
allways think that i am right
have an ansewer to everything
and allways have to have
the last
word

my son shows me who i once was

i show my son a picture
of myself
aged 3
whos this huddie
i ask
huddie
he says
and
i laugh
lift him to my arms
put my lips to his golden hair
and breath him
and kiss the back of his kneck
he kicks and stuggles
i put him down
and he runs up the corridoor
and back down again calling
- papa papa
and jumps back into my arms

i feel the life darting within him
and a feeling of such joy and sadness
struggles up from my chest
that it threatens to strangle me

and
then
to imagin a broad-sword in my hand
and suddenly – with one blow -
i take off the head of norman
the 42 year old man
who abused me

and
i marvel that such love and anger
is within me
then celibrate
for i know that i after all am human
and
am now a man

POLICE

my fathers gift

for every reason you hated me
i will love you

becouse
you had to break the boils
that swarmed across
my legs and back
becouse
my shit stank to high heaven
becouse
i couldnt read and rite
and i wouldnt speak properly
becouse
i was bludy thick
and had bad teeth
becouse
my hair looked like
a savages
and i pissed the bed
and becouse
i hung round with criminels
who broke in and stole your
naked lady bottle opener
and the miserly 40 quid
you gave the old girl every month
to keep us and your silly house

becouse you
never spoke with me
or held me
or said you loved me
i will love you
and
love my son

so this is your hidden gift

tai chi

listen
i shout at my mother
- its not the man who throws a stone
into a pool of water
and makes ripples
who is remarkable
its the man who throws a stone
into a pool of water
and there are no ripples
no! my mother shouts
sitting up in her chair
you have to make waves
in this world!

i am fourteen
and there is no way that
my mother
is going to understand
the gentleness of
the chinese art of tai chi
so standing
i kick the table
across the room
and
throw my half drunk can
of ginger beer
up the wall
and when i look up
my father is stood there
in the doorway
his white ganex mac
gleaming
in the darkness
his brolly furlled
tightly
in his hand

**i wear broken shoes
in the houses of prostitutes**

presume that i am guilty
for sure i am arrogant
and put myself before others

it is also true that i pray for myslf
and have worn broken shoes
in the houses of prostitutes

nite times
i rite lines against
my self and my enimys
i love to force life to a painful point
with poetry that is not poetry
but revenge

it should also be taken
into account
that at 17
i was convicted of stealling a jar
of country born setting jell
from boots the chemists
it is also true that
after my fathers arrest
i set my girlfriends
hair on fire
and
had a bank account
under the name of
kurt schwitters

strangly proud

it
is possible that
i enjoyed being sexualy abused
at the age of 9
and
did there after
maliciously wet the bed
purely to keep my mother
at werk nite and day
washing piss soaked
sheets

it should also be known
that in 1973 i kicked a bucket
of burning creasoat
up my fathers newly painted
chiminy breast
indirctly killing off of a large section
of his beloved lawn
and
after at first denying all knowlge
of this act
i then shamlessly said that
i was sorry
when i definetly
was not

in my early teens
i then went on to experiment
with explosives
drink from an illigal still
vanderlize building sites
burn down fields of corn
and
pray to god for the death
of my father
and brother

all of this
has been seen thru
the distorting lense of this
so called poet
who is too full of vanity
to be belived
and
for all these things
i am truely sorry
but also
strangly
proud

at midnite i will say i love you

in this house tonite
insects dance
the walls holding up the nite
and spyders
viberate in their webs
laughing

liein benith
the old pump organ
is the mumified corps
of a poisoned mouse
killed
by an ex girlfriend

all i have left to say
is that i am sorry
or rather
that i am angry that
you think that
i should say
that i am sorry
but
i am sorry

it is true
that the furniture
is busted
and the carpets are filthy
but i dont want to
worry about furniture
or muddy feet
or hoovering
or head aches
or moskito bites

or the kings
and queens
of
art
and
fashion

do you know something
next doors cat
used to come and
and sit on my shoulders
whilest i was riting
she was black and friendly
called tibs
but i renamed her
mister tibbs
then she got fleas
and the old girlfriend
banished her
from the house
next
the phone shivers
into life
and
afraid of aloness
i ansewer

it is midnite
and
i will say that
i love you
even if
i have to lie

i give myself to them all

i walk towards this nite
towards the drunkards
and the lost
towards the sluts
and the broken of
hart
in hard bitten bars
between dog-ends and bad scotch
sucking on bitter cigars
and dreams of bitter whores
and i give myself to you all
to these piss soaked walls
and kicked in doors

you of purple breath
you of painted flesh
you of dusky flesh
you of hated tits and arses
come be in my poems
for ive come to write you all
you shit eaters
and you beaten
you ridiculed and despised
yes you espesherly
come bring your voices
and we will walk arm in arm
thru this whore of a town
towards the stinking river
and the dawn
and
our dreams shall prove no less poetic
our love no less true
and our kisses be as sweet
as dog rose

for here all are welcome

monkys in space

my nanna lewis used to give us
these brookbond tea cards
a serris on the conquest of space
on the front were paintings of little dogs
and monkys

i got nanna lewis to read out the
biographys on the backs of the cards
i was so excited to lern that dogs and monkys were
now flying rockets
she told me their names and the dates of
their missions

where are they now
i asked
still in space i supose
when are they coming back
i dont know angel i dont think they are coming back
why not
the rockets only go one way
why didnt they go and resque them
i ask
becouse theyer dead
says my brother

the man who thought he would never be a father is a father

the man who thought he would never be a father
is a father
the man who thought he would never hold a child in
his arms
holds a child in his arms
holds him to his aching hart

and when i hold you
and perseve you in your open wounder of the world
it is allmost to painful for me
i too remember being as open and blessed as you
and every movement of your breath
i too remember making that movement
and the movements are one

and every pain of parting
with your mother
i too remember the pain of that parting
with my mother
when i see the golden light that surrounds you
i too remember that golden light and i understand why
my nanna lewis called me 'her angel'

and when i hold you in these supple arms
i realise that i too hold myself
every gentlle part of your buti
is my buti
your eyes that carry no darkness
are my eyes
your lips that want to know every sensation
are my lips
and as i cradle you to my chest
my heart shudders
and
i think of life and death
and wounder at how these two mysterys are linked
hand in hand
and think of what special promiss
i want to give you

that promis is of my undying love
which my father could never give to me
but which flows from me to you so painfully and so easyly
these are my feelings becouse i am your father
the man who never thought he would be a father

it is the poets job

to remain forever outside
and forever ridiculed

to alenate his family and friends
to be petty
and jelliose
and spitful

to fail missrably
show his soft underbelly
and grin like an idiot
to be like jesus christ
judas
and the buddha

to chase his own tail
avoid prizes
accolaydes
and
rewards
and never become celibrated

car alarms weep for me in the nite

thats how its allways been
no matter how many years pass

walking these streets
i drew pictures of mad dictators
on the backs of ciggaret packets
visited
by
ex-girlfriends and my astranged father
i tryed not to be a nuesence to
shoppers
tourists
or general passers by

even now
kids still taunt me
on account
of the way i dress
my hair falls over my brow
and they shout
- hitler
at me
but
theyve got the rong man

i see myself in a shop window
and i look like ive just landed
it scears me to realise that i will allways
feel new here

the shed

my car is a 68 volvo estate
given me by my brother
painted seaweed green
drinks a gallon of oil a week
he hands over the keys
theres a special way of opening the bonnit
he tells me
and the back door dosnt lock
and the rear window
dosnt wind up
yourll have to jam it with something
heres a spear key
if you can find anyone who still cuts them
get more cut
becouse they snap off in the ignition
i keep a spair in the ashe tray
in case of imergences
get some gaffer tape
cos the back number plates almost off
and yourll need a plastic bag over your leg
cos the rain leeks in round the wind shield
and it dips over the exsalerator
and when you put in the petrol
only fill it a quarter full
otherwise the tank leeks

other than that
it goes pritty good
oh yes
and its called the shed

ps the drivers side rear lite is smashed out and taped
over with a red malteaser packet

ants moths and picaso

little ones
you have come to visit
you love to be near man
and
nest beneith warm concreat
cracked paths are your favorite
you
also walk up the sides of trees
your tiny feet stepping close to
the powdery wings of moths

you carry your dead friends
on your heads
and
once i saw five of you draging
a dead spyder
under a broken
paving slab to be eaten
by your hungry clan

it is said that on seeing dazzel-painted trucks
driving thru the streets of paris during the great war
picaso pointed and exclaimed
'we (the cubists) are responsble for that'
he didnt mention moths
or zebras at all
thats how we know that he was full of himself

tattoo

in 1966
huddled in my fathers mirror dingy
we sailed off seasalter and shellness

i wore an old cork life-jackett that diddnt fit
and ducked as the boom swung drunkenly above my head
so as to be like my grandad
i got my father to draw tattoos on my fore arms
with felt-tip pens
evey five minits i peeped up my sleeves to see
if the salt spray had washed them off
the red sails boombed
and my father shouted orders
i watched his bearded face
his eyes looking angrly at the sea

when we got ashore my father bought a trombone
for 25 pounds off a man
who was
sexualy abusing me

2

sitting in my fathers
back garden in the stinging sun
a fresh tattoo on my shoulder
and ciggaret burns
littering my fore arms
my father stands angryly over me
i dont know how you can do that to yourself
he says
then turns and walks away

here-boys lead

my nanna lewis brought me and my brother
those belts after visiting
our uncle in canada
there were pictures of red indians
galloping on horse back painted all round them
and i ran out into the garden whooping

after a year or so mine got too small
so it got chucked out
but my elder brothers became
the lead for my stray dog
here-boy

here-boys been dead 18 years now
but i wear the belt again
you can see the tooth marks were he
used to chew on it
and the pictures of red indians have all worn away

the last of my childhood

a photograph
taken by my father
sometime in the mid sixties
i sit on the top of a pile of shingle
on sea salter beach
giving the thumbs up with a bandaged thumb
on my feet are my scuffed
black slip-on plimsoles
and my 'tufty club' road safty badge
is pinned to my chest
i must be about 6 or 7 years old

this is one of the last photographs
of my childhood
shortly after this my father left us
and there were no more
family holidays

then one day in the mid 70s my father came home
gathered all of the family photographs
cleared the shelfs of the pornography we'd stolen from
him
took our collection of old 45's
and built a bonfire
in the back yard

the stench of burning plastic
drifted across the lawn
as he emptied a suit-case full of negatives
into the flames
i watched him from my bedroom window

in the morning the fire was still smouldering
and my father was gone
i walked over to the embers
toed the lake of hard melted vinyl
and hated this man
who had never spoken to me
and was now intent on destroying
the last of my childhood

the day is begging for your kiss

i will be waiting outside the old school gates
where you came that day to abduct me
i will have no gun concealed in my pocket
just my harmless white fist

if you here the birds singing
think of me
of how you wanted to take
me to the woods
and kill me
if you see matted hair in the plug hole
think of me
if you see a car go past
think of me
or a plain in the sky
or trees
or grass
or 2 dogs fighting
or fucking
or a childs face at a window
that will be good
or
as you look at the backs of your old hands
think of me
becouse
i am still here
and though in your mind
i am still only a child
i am not a sex object
but a man

the reluctant human being (every button of my life)

1

she wishes to leave me
and i wish to leave her
yet she loves me
and i strangly love her

but my lust for other women
and her denial of my malenes
fills my head with hate and sorrow

plucking up courarge
i turn to her in bed and tell her
that i just want to be with a woman
who wants me
who desires me for what i am
rather than hates me for it

2

if you think that i can live
for 3 days without sex
then i am a different animal
than you imagin

but you want me to last 2 weeks
3 weeks
4 weeks
you can live without sex
you tell me it dosnt bother you

so now my life really has come
to an end

3

im sick of my sexual desires
and sick of you fighting me off
in the middle of each nite

im sick of your goodness
and your beutiful blond hair
that is intangled round
every button of my life

im sick of the sunlite
and this terrible lonlyness
which everybody tells me
i shouldnt have

4

again im walking home
alone
in the nite time
speaking to a god who surrounds me
but dosnt answer

still unknowing of myself
and bringing missery to my companions
who i say that i love
but in truth
i dont know the meaning
of the word
i stumble on

5

on the way home tonite
there was a large brested
ginger-haired girl
kneeling in a bush crying

6
at midnite
i walk to the park
and climb into the lower limbs
of a horse chestnut tree

the apparent bravery of my youth
is gone
and i struggle to get a meer
30ft above the ground
the blackness of the shadows below
frighten me
and
i realise that i am not
after all going
to sleep the nite aloft
and let my ex girlfriend
belive that i am dead

7
i sleep in graveyards with kings

i touched a childs head today
placed my hand to her braids
'dont touch me' she said
and looked at me with
the beutiful slanting eyes
of my ex-girlfriend

i have always wanted children
but have been
to sceared to utter it

8

the river is beutifull
becouse it is posionus
as is life
becouse of death
and silence
becouse of words
and darkness
becouse of lite

on a plain
from america
a black girl
sitting next to me
tells me that
state murder
is sanctioned by god
and that paul
is the voice of the
living mercyfull jesus

i need jesus
i tell her
but a jesus that
dosnt love murder

9

i squat on this hillside
above the black river
and deficate
a newspaper
flutters in the
bushes and startles me
once again
i am contemplating suiside
but no angels visit me

10

i need to know who i am
and why i am
i take off my cloaths
and walk alone in the darkness

bellow me
cars pass thru the nite town

i am 39 years of age
and once again am
playing hide and seek
with a police car at
1.45 am

11

this poem is in loving
memory of the child
i alowed my girlfriend
to abort
cowedly leaving her
the decission
saying
i would go along with
whatever were her wishes

rather than making a demand
for life
i allowed murder

no wounder that my dreams
are haunted
and littered with the graves
of my victims

i am the boss of all
english riters

listen to me
i dont walk in straight lines
i am rude
(not only to winners
but also the losers)

my style is off target and amiturish
bad feelings run thru me
friends tell me that my farts smell like a rotten compost
heap
has fallen out my arse

i examin molicules
in the breath of
ants

novelists
hate me
as would poets and artists
if only they could be bothered to find out who i am

i celibrate
mistakes and full stops
becouse god and christ
are
not feasting in the halls
of the celibrated
but
waighting
to step from the mouths
of the damned
and
the lost

the wounded poet

who is meaner
funnier
and
more perverse than me
who is so childlike
so far seeing
and
narrower
than myself
who is so desscreet
so indecent
and such a blabber mouth

who is more crewl
and
loving
who could be as hard
and sentimental
who is so much in need
of uplifting and praise
whos ego so rampant
yet self seen

what poet can better me
in battle
and where is there a finner
more compleat artist
than myself

who
in the history of the world
has ever seen themselfs so low
in theyer own estermations
or been so bostful
impudent
and shy

who has been so cut from god
yet joined with god
who has asked so many fine questions
and supplied such sparkling answers

who has embraced so many women
and fellows
and helped so many lost poets

who has made such a
sumptious banquet of himself
beqithed his bones
to the yet-to-be-born
made such a feast of his flesh for the angry
the impoverished of soul
and haters
of simple art

the man with the gallows eyes

i see love
from these gallows eyes
i see children play
and
birds on the wing
and
who needs art gallerys when youve got nature
busted twigs
a fat slug
bright leaf jewls
and benith
wrestling ants
pea-bugs
and
spyders

oh yes
i see death everywhere
from these gallows eyes
the fact that i ripped out my stomach lineing
with cheap whisky
and
everyday i meet
my own disgust
and
you
too
must see your own face
in these gallows eyes

i am here to build jurrusolom

i am the best friend of your werst enimy
i am tooth ache
and
the sum totle of all of your dreams
i am the green hills
and
the builder of endless motorways

i am the kisser of purple–lipped woman
who hate men
i am the man who sold you ice creams as a child
whilest singing 'make me a sargent'

i am the hand of the man who molested me
i am my fathers wife as he beats her up
i am my worried mother suckling me
and
telling me i must conform or be crushed
i am the drunk who pissed himself whilest asking
you for the price of cup of tea
i am my father lying cheating and denying
i am the man you pushed out of the way
to arrive home 30 seconds earlyer

i am a knight of honour who sets girls hair alight
i am the killer of black birds and undertaker to
dead mice
i am the face of all the dead who ever lived in the
history of the world
i am the grandchild who tells his grandparents
that their son is in prison
i am the goader of dogs and monkys

i am the son whos father is
disgusted with him
it was me who stole your suit
and kicked creasoat up your wall
i am the luftwaffa and destroyer of inner-city inishatives
i am the lover of crack prostitutes
i am the man who informed the police of your
whereabouts
it was me who rotted you garden gate
and
snaped your shoe laces
i am the man killed whilest riding on his bicycle

i am the friend of the duplisitus
and champanion of the fake
i am the sodermised corps of a child
found in lite undergroth
the corps dreged from the sea
i am the missing husband who
hanged himself
i invented sythaliss

i am all my girlfriends who hated me
i am the man caught drinking his own sperm
i am the man who held you when no one else would
i despise everything about you and your family
i sit next to god

i am the moth that taught piccaso
it was me who had sex with your pet dog
i have stolen your weding ring
and
dropped it behind an old dresser

i am the stranger you saw kissing
your mother
i am the man who painted all the
werst paintings in the world
and
sold them as great art
i am the teacher who made
your childhood a living hell

i kiss your bad teeth and stinking mouth
i will burn all your love letters
in the grate
and
tell you i hate you
i will be the only person to remember you
when you are ded

i am here to build jurusollom

i am the un corrected

becouse
i cant spell
and
refuse to show off
with cheep tricks
and
still allow myself to paint
like a monky
i
am not elivated

fear me

becouse
i have no certificates
refused to be educated
and
my riting style is free
true
and easy
yet
i have ritten novels
that disgust the sences
i
am not elevated

fear me

i
am gloryiously
un corrected
and will
be coming for you
next

deaths
head
moth

a nite visiter
came to
the mad house

the artist
looked in wounder
at its colours of amazing distinction
black
gray
cloudy white
tinged with carmine
or vaguely shading off
into olive green

it was a pity
he
had to kill it to paint it
opening his cupped hands
he
flicked its head with his
finger
the moth emited a loud squeek
and fell silent

he arranged it on the nite stand
opening out its powderery wings
he painted feverisly
thru the nite

the beastie was so butiful

you moth
are
known as
the severer of the thread of life
the wandering death birds cry
your voice of angish
has been likened
to the
moaning
of
grief stricken children
you honey robber

the painting finished
the artist
sent it along
to his younger brother
thou
the
moths visit
told him
that
nither of them
were
long for this world

the genious is ready for life

in fear of baldness
i have purchesed
a chinese devise
that sends electrical currents
threw
the acupunture points
in my scull

also
my sperm count is low
and
i have lower back pains
due to masterbating
like the devil

my left groin aches
and
the pain shoots
down my left buttock
and
into my leg

in my youth
i imagined a day when
i would
be somehow
magicaly whole
my wiskers would
no longer
grow patchey
and
my genious be recognised
and
so
i would
at last
be ready for life

in hand knitted socks

in hand knitted
socks
i walk the beachs at winter time

today i painted 2 pictures
after van gogh
sun flowers
and
the
church at auvers

‘this
is certanly
not the way
for a serrious artist
to behave’
i tell my wife
‘not if he wishes to be
elivated
and
taken
serriously’

we look out to sea
across the fog bound estery
i fear no one
i tell her
and
will
hand my enimys
this
butiful loaded revolver

the lion tamer
of boundary rd

women suffering from
alapicia
grin enviously
at my head of silken hair
school children
admire
my masterfull
drawing
skills
and drunks
and
the lost
oggle me with eyes like grapes
sure that i am a wise
and hate them

boys with bum-fluth
covert my mustashes
dogs on the street
hang their red tungs
salivating
over my level
of spiritual development
and
aspiring poets are simply
bowled over
by my
ryhme
spelling
and
collection
of
hats

convicted
murderers cannot comprhend
the screaming pitch of my anger
and
the suisidle
hate me
for
my calmness
and aqinimity

virgins
and
the depraved
hover longingly
over my sexual exploits
and
even
the famouse
are jellious
and
wish that they
could be as
un-famouse as me

meanwhile
i stryed down boundary rd
and
the pussy cats on the street
cower benith
motor cars
convinced
that
i am a mighty lion taimer

it is simple

do not strive to
paint
do not strive to
rite
do not strive for
postion
do not stive for
rewards
do not strive to
for power
do not strive
for love

un-do painting
un-do riting
un-do life

the first green horse
god has made

driving
towards a pink sky
we
pull into the petroll station
i check the oil
and buy 12 pounds worth of petrol
on account that you cant fill the tank becouse
theres a leek half ways up

huddie sits in the car
with my wife julie
and i go in
and
pay

climbing back in
huddie tells me
i saw a green horse running papa
a green one really? now theyer unussual
it was wearing a green coat
explains julie
huddie shakes his head
no it wasnt it was green
it must be the first green horse
god has ever made

a message to the ants

come visit my poems
at nite
your armys are legion
children want to see you
make war
and
like them
you love suger

you walk
up the sides of trees
milk aphieds like cattle
and your eggs
are
food for goldfish

with boiling water
magnifying glass
and
liter fuel
i killed so many of you
when i was a child
now i beg your forgivness

wood pecker

she said thered be eagles
we drove through new housing
developments
that she said wernt there
last year

we park
and
start up towards the mountain
i was surprized
by the tarmac paths
and
she got angry
becouse
i comented on them

she gave me
the silent treatment
striding off in front
taking mighty strydes
i
had to run to keep up with her
i asked her to slow down
and
she told me she was stronger than
i was

she
said thered be eagles
but there wasnt

we have war
becouse
we love war

becouse we
want to push
to the front
and
have
all the prizes
to ourselfs

becouse love
is not enough
nor
are
new cars
or out of town shopping complexes
or mobile phone
of sourround-a-sound sterios
or 60 inch telivision screens
or ready prepaired meals
or hollidays in other peoples missery
or jesus
or budha
or being able to eat smoke and drink ourselfs to death
then cry that our hospitals are all shit

becouse
we need
to feel slighted
and
peeved
by the least
inconvenence
of the day
becouse the sun is not right
or our shoelaces are too tight

or
becouse
we hate our mothers
or our fathers
or our wifes
or our sisters
or our brothers
or techers for failing us
or people for failing us
or husbands for leaving us
or the sky
or the rain
or our bosses
or our children
or our werk mates
or pedophiles
or the mad
or car drivers
or pedestrians
or people on bikes
or people wearing the rong type of hats
or the rong shoes
or smoking cigarets
or not smoking cigarets
or drinking
or not drinking
or foregners
or faceists
or policeman
or peace marchers
but
ultimatly
ourselfs

where excentrics fear to tread

in this town
where
the gray faces of 15 year old whores
lite the nite streets

and
drunken mothers
with babes in arms
spit on the backs of hunched backed women
on nite buses
who are then in turn
beaten around the head with bottles

and
in multi story car parks
where rubber johnnys are spilled to the ground
and squadies have their ears bitten off
and spitten to the ground
and lovers leap
and
the sky smashes into the hillsides

and
all the while
there is still meraclious
silence
and peace
and space and joy

where
van gogh once stepped
and
excentrics fear to tread

love the jaws of the lion

if you love poetry
you must hate poetry
if you love art
you must hate art

if you love beuti
you must hate butie
if you love man
you must hate man

if you love laughter
you must hate laughter
if you love the forest at nite time
you must hate the forest at nite time

if you love the lion
you must
love the jaws
about to eat you

knight of the sad face

in this town
where
i
have lost
several teeth
a note book containg poetry
of a personal nature
the paintings of my youth
3 girlfriends
a
pocketfull
of
lose change
my fathers
yellow hair
my claim to genius
a small screw
a pair of stollen sissors
reasons
belieth
and
the buttons off my overcoat

i have found
a piece of cheap jewelry
on a hillside
belonging to a cryying
indian girl
afraid of being beaten by her mother

hearing her sobs
i stand walk 20 paces
look down
and there it is at my feet
i
pick up the bracelet
call to her
and
drop it glinting into her smiling palm
she turns and runs laughing to her friends
all dressed in shimmering saris

they leave the field
and
i am left looking after them
this knight of the sad face

i am still the poet
of
herpis sores
and
eurgency

i have not grown
i am still the poet
of herpis sores and eurgency

the poet of indiscresions
of blindness
and
weekness
petty revenge
and
jellousey

i hold onto my black island
and
i was allways
the poet
of forgivness
and
god
as i kissed the prostiotuets mouth

i am a knight of honour

yes
i set lite to your hair
and
yes
i punched you in the jaw
and
yes
i got married behind your back
and
yes
i rote those awful poems about us
of our nites of passion
and how mean spirited you were
and
yes
i destroyed the only 3 love letters
that i ever sent you
(i broke into your flat whilest you pretended
to be living on a barge in amsterdam
and burnt them in the fire place)
and
yes
i refused to marry you
and settle down and have children
and
yes
i picked you up by the stomach
and thru you across
the floor
and
you lost a child
that you never told me you were
carrying

and yes i gave you a dose of
gohnareah
when i slept with that
german prostitute
and yes i refused to have sex with you
and
yes
i slept with that japanese girl
begging her to save me from the
otterman empire
and
when you asked me to lie
i did my best to lie
and
yes
i spoke with that
idiotic newspaper
when you swore at me not to
but
sweet hart
i never
punched you as hard as i let you
punch me
nor have i
for the sake of succsses
denied you
as you have
denied me
or lied like you lie

but
if one day
you should need a friend
who dosnt agree with you
who
will tell you
when you are a bully
a big mouth
and a fool
who has listend to your
fears
and helped you when you split up with your boyfriends
and given you time
and money
when you had none
and listened
when you wanted to kill yourself
i am here
and
will
never
let you down
for
i am a knight of honour

you who have allways been with me
and have allways held me
i right this poem to you across the nite
that dosnt seperate us
but joins us

you are the spirit of all women
your name was wisperd to me
in the sleep befor birth
and it will be upon my lips
when i pass from this life
and
into realms unimaginable

you who have allways been with me
and have have allways held me
i likewise will allways be with you
and
will allways hold you

even in the lonlyness
and
abusess of my childhood
you were still somhow with me

thou you wernt yet born
you surrounded me like the good air
and protected me
covering
my body in sweet
kisses
likewise
i protect you
and cover your body
in sweet kisses

i speak to lonly artists

do you really think that i care if i sell
a painting or not? i answer - i care not!

i speak to lonly artists in the nite
across time
the desperate young men and women
not yet born
and those already dead
i offer them hope
joy and lite
i tell them not to fret
paint your pictures
fame is worth nought!
i hold them all to me
and they in turn hold me

i whisper down the centuries
speaking words into the wombs
of their butiful mothers
who give life for no other reason
than that
god gives life and the flowers must
bloom

i speak to the harts
of lost children
and i bring good news
do not hate yourselfs but love
yourselfs
do not mock your abusive fatheres
and weeping mothers
but love their weakness
do not down cheap whisky
and burn a hole in your guts
but to love your beutiful guts

you artist down the centrys
the gutter is a fine place to find
yourself
but not a place to live
you are my children
or rather
we are brothers
and sisters
but allow me to call you my children
becouse i love you so
now climb out and paint with
your brushes
bring forth your abilities or die
like slaves

do i care that my voice is lost in
the gibbering
crowds
in the noise of art fashion and
finance?
i ansewer cheerfully - i cear not

because
my memory is allready sacred
amongst my children
amongst those yet to be born
those who will love me and i in turn
will love them

i comune with the souls of dead
artists
in spirit not only here and now
but that spans all the ages of man
i speak with the un-holy and lost
with the godless and shamefull
those
who only in death do the cowards
lift up
and champion

i speak with lonly artists
in colours that are sound
on inner planes
we are found
we are as one
we celebrate
for the living soul of man has allwas
been mocked for its inarticulet
mumblings and kingship to idiocy

speaking with the yet to be born
and
embracing and loveing them all
i urge them onwards
towards life
telling them to have no fear and to
show
their glorious spirit
becouse the young love love
and they in turn urge me to make
this utterence

i commune with old ghosts
ghosts
i say
do not fret that you were ever
denouced
missunderstood or ignored by
your age
this is not your failer but your strength
this is the nature of our brotherhood
our comunity
it has allways been so
so pick up your pencils
be never vengfull
and carry the torch to the next
generation
of impoverished underdogs
and
smile on them in love

Born in 1959 in Chatham, Kent. Billy Childish left Secondary education at 16 an undiagnosed dyslexic. Refused an interview at the local art school he entered the Naval Dockyard at Chatham as an apprentice stonemason. During the following six months (the artist's only prolonged period of employment) he produced some six hundred drawings in 'the tea huts of hell'. On the basis of this work he was accepted into St Martin's School of Art to study painting. However, his acceptance was short-lived and before completing the course he was expelled for writing what was termed "The worst type of toilet wall humour". Childish then spent some 12 years painting on the dole, developing his own highly personal writing style and producing his art independently.